The **Essential** Buyer's Guide

JAGUAR/DAIMLER
XJ6, XJ12
& SOVEREIGN

All Jaguar/Daimler/VDP Series 1, 2 & 3
models 1968 to 1992

Your marque expert: Peter Crespin

GH00503685

VELOCE PUBLISHING
THE PUBLISHER OF FINE AUTOMOTIVE BOOKS

The Essential Buyer's Guide Series

www.veloce.co.uk

First published in June 2007. Reprinted in November 2014 and April 2020 by Veloce Publishing Limited, Veloce House, Parkway Farm Business Park, Middle Farm Way, Poundbury, Dorchester DT1 3AR, England. Tel 01305 260068 / Fax 01305 268864 / e-mail info@veloce.co.uk / web www.veloce.co.uk or www.velocebooks.com. ISBN: 978-1-845841-19-5/UPC 6-36847-04119-9

Introduction & thanks

– the purpose of this book

What this book offers

This book can't hope to deal with the large XJ model range in great depth, even restricting its range to 1968-1986, but it does show you the main things to watch out for when checking an XJ for potential purchase. It's small enough to take with you when inspecting a car, and detailed enough to help you avoid buying a bad example, but cannot do these marvellous cars full justice.

The XJ6 can be traced back to a project aimed at developing a larger E-type for the American market. Although by the time it was launched in 1968 it was very definitely a luxury saloon not a sports car, it nevertheless possessed class-leading handling, performance, road-holding and refinement that can be traced back to the giant leap forward represented by the E-type seven years earlier.

The XJ range rapidly became Jaguar's only saloon range and sold extremely well, with the XJ12 version being hailed as probably the best car in the world by more than one reviewer. The XJ saw Jaguar through the lean years of poor build quality during the British Leyland era, and formed the basis for John Egan's privatization and quality revival. It lasted right through to Ford ownership in 1989 and, though the 6-cylinder range had been surpassed by the XJ40, the much-respected Series 3 V12s ran for 3 more years, such was the demand for this superlative car whilst Jaguar modified the XJ40 to take the iconic V12 in the 1993/94 model years.

Even today, a good XJ will take its owner far and fast (and smoothly), making them practical propositions for modern roads and supremely addictive to drive, especially in V12 form.

With some 400,000 produced over almost 25 years, there are plenty of good-value survivors to choose from and you can afford to be fussy. Enjoy the hunt!

Acknowledgements

This book has only been possible because many XJ owners in the UK and overseas supplied pictures and details of their cars and ownership experiences. Special thanks are due to Dr Gregory Andrachuck, Doug Dwyer, Robert Wilkinson, Richard Kan, Ken Cantor, Eric Feron, Zoli Kovacs, Nick Johanssen, and many others.

Peter Crespin
Gaithersburg, Maryland

*(See the Veloce 6-cylinder E-type Buyer's Guides for the six-cylinder and V12 cars respectively).

Contents

The Essential Buyer's Guide™ currency
At the time of publication a BG unit of currency "●" equals approximately £1.00/US$1.24/Euro 1.14. Please adjust to suit current exchange rates using Sterling as the base currency.

1 Is it the right car for you?
– marriage guidance

Tall and short drivers
All XJs have reclining seats, with lumbar adjustment on Series 3s (S3), and electric height adjustment on the top S3 models. All have reach-adjustable steering and suit a diversity of drivers, with long wheelbase models very roomy in the rear. Headrests arrived with late Series 1 cars but are too low for long-bodied drivers. Headroom is good, even if a factory electric sunroof is fitted. Early cars had 16-inch steering wheels, but the later 15-inch wheel offers more thigh room.

Weight of controls
All XJs have power steering which is lighter than modern cars but encourages a relaxed, fingertip, 'period' driving style, and is certainly helpful in town driving, if a little low-geared for fast roads. Most XJs are automatics, but manual cars have a reasonable clutch and good gearchange. All XJs use multi-piston brake calipers which are fine for modern driving, though needing firm pedal pressure and not as sharp as modern discs. The under-dash handbrake can require a good pull to hold the car, but if properly adjusted it is adequate. Beware leaving it on, however.

Plenty of room for most shapes and sizes.

Will it fit the garage?
Length* (SWB and Coupé): 4815mm/189.5in
(LWB): 4945mm/194.7in
Width 1770mm/69.7in
Height 1374mm/54.1in

* North American models, especially S2 and 3, were longer by about 127mm/5in because of deep impact-resistant bumpers.

Oddment tray and large wheel of S1 intrude slightly.

Interior space
Even the short wheelbase cars are broad and will seat three in the back easiy, though two will always be more comfortable with the arm rest down. Rear seat knee room is fair in short wheelbase cars even with the front seats well back, but the long wheelbase cars will hold four tall people without problems, and five in reasonable comfort. The higher S3 roofline means rear headroom is best in these cars. Many Daimler/Vanden Plas models have sculpted rear seats designed for two people, although three can fit.

More room in later S3. Note velour seats.

Luggage capacity
All models have generous boot space, though it is long and wide but shallow,

Good headroom in Avon convertible!

Wide but shallow boot space of late S3.

especially at the rear; the luggage has to be unpacked to reach the spare wheel. All doors have generous

oddment bins, and the front armrest conceals a sizeable cubby box, with a small shelf above the centre console. A lockable glovebox with fitted vanity mirror completes the luggage arrangements, apart

from trays under the dash on Series 1 cars and a cubby in the rear centre armrest on Vanden Plas and late Daimlers. Some models had magazine pockets in the back of the front seats.

Roomy long wheelbase Daimler.

Running costs

XJ fuel consumption increases with engine size, though all

are thirsty. Early V12s use a lot of fuel, and even the better late V12s still drink heavily. Despite this they are addictive to drive and the larger-engined cars need to be driven for good distances to get properly warm. For those wishing to use their XJ as daily or regular year-round transport (which the car is perfectly capable of), a conversion to liquefied gas fuel reduces costs and pollution, at the cost of boot space unless you run with a round tank and no spare wheel.

Generous rear room, even in 2-door.

Depending on transmission, driving style and gearing you'll get around

LWB car, short wheelbase garage.

11-15mpg (Imperial) from a V12 (3-4mpg more from a later HE engine), less if pressing on. The 4.2-litre carburettor cars give 15-19mpg with the 3.4 reaching the low twenties and the 2.8 doing slightly better, but not by much. Being classic cars, they generally require servicing by time as well as mileage, so that annual or twice-yearly oil changes may be called for, which are not cheap at over 8-litres/17.5 US pints for the sixes, and around 9- to 11-litres (19-23 US pints) for the twelves, depending on series.

Much servicing is DIY but many owners pay for specialist work, as with any modern car. Of the consumables, apart from oil volumes, only the fitting/adjustment of handbrake or rear disc pads is unusually expensive. Valve clearances are time-consuming to adjust but rarely need doing, once set up.

Useability

XJs were always superb driver's cars, and are still capable of crossing continents or city centres in equal style. You may well come to prefer driving your XJ to driving your normal car. The smallest-engined models are not quick, especially fully loaded, but they are better than many others in their time and, from the 3.4 upwards, they are smooth and swift and still respectable today. Short, infrequent trips are much harder on the car than regular use and long runs where the big engine can warm up fully and heat the cabin. Many XJs have air conditioning fitted, which uses more fuel but makes it possible to arrive at a business or social appointment looking fresh.

Parts availability

There are many specialists who can supply almost every part new (many still made by Jaguar) except for some trim for rarer models. The engines outlasted the XJ by being used in the Daimler limousines, and the 5.3 V12 survived until 1993 when it became the 6.0-litre (though many later spares don't interchange).

Aftermarket and secondhand spares availabilities are also excellent.

Parts cost

XJs aren't as expensive as some other high-end cars but the size/complexity and high levels of trim mean they are dearer than more modest classics. Leather interiors and a full re-trim are expensive but compared to modern cars spares prices overall are reasonable. Service can involve large labour bills for fitting some parts.

Insurance

As large-engined prestige cars, XJs are not the cheapest to insure but classic policies are reasonable in almost all cases. Many insurers require an immobilizer to be fitted. Get several quotes and investigate limited-mileage policies to keep costs down. If restoring your own car, consider insurance during storage, which may take many months or even years.

Investment potential

XJs are not rare cars and not an ideal investment due to the much lower resale values than, say, E-types or the XK sports cars. The chance of making a significant profit are remote, since restoration costs are close to those of the dearer cars and a full restoration invariably costs more than the car is worth and many have been lost to 'clunker' programmes. In terms of smiles per mile, however, they are great value.

Alternatives

Hardly anything compares, especially to the 12s. They were amongst the best cars in the world when they were new and few classics afterwards were much better. Most alternatives would be German, French or American luxury cars, or the occasional Rolls-Royce or Bentley (which hardly ever come both cheap and healthy). Contemporary BMW and Mercedes cars are rivals to the saloons, and some Mercedes and BMW coupés competed with the two-door XJs. Italian 12-cylinder exotica were rarely anything but highly-strung GT or sports cars, and are very expensive to buy and maintain. Some Rover models compare, and a few top-end Humbers, with the range-topping Fords and Citroëns not really in the same league. One other 2-door sporting/grand touring 12-cylinder car would be the Jaguar XJ-S. 8-cylinder options might be Lincoln, Cadillac, Aston Martin, or Jensen.

2 Cost considerations
– affordable, or a money pit?

Purchase price

No XJ is really expensive, compared to some other Jaguar classics. Therefore, even the best cars are comparatively affordable, though dearer than less impressive makes. Those who want a really good car should look at the top of the market and spend more initially, to have a more reliable and durable vehicle from the start. Others, who are merely looking for a taste of the XJ experience, and will settle for a car to give them a couple of seasons of fun before selling or restoring, can afford to buy at the bottom of the market for complete, roadworthy, or almost roadworthy, cars. Other options are paying good money for a near complete refurbished vehicle to be finished off, or buying a cheap model in need of total restoration, which will probably work out more expensive later.

Concours standard takes effort.

Affordable to run?

For XJs to be used regularly it's important to factor in fuel, servicing, consumables and insurance costs when deciding whether the car will be affordable to run. Modern cars suffer depreciation but low running costs. XJs are generally the opposite and should at least hold their value. If you want a car that will go on for year after year with nothing more than oil, water and fuel then you are underestimating the commitment of owning a large classic which wasn't cheap to run when it was new, and will not be cheap to run 20-30 years later.

Manual choke-converted daily driver.

Price bands

If you're looking for an excellent show car you'll need to spend more than £5000-£6000 – perhaps significantly more. A car which is perfectly respectable for day-to-day use, but not so spotless that you daren't put lots of miles on it, will cost something around £2000-£3000. Bargain cars, especially if they have just passed inspection, can be had for £1000-£2000, but there are also cars below that which could give a year's service with few major outlays. Because the XJ cars are the most common Jaguars, there is the option of buying a different

Gas conversion cuts fuel bills.

cheap car every season and spending money only on running repairs, rather than actually investing in upgrades or a proper restoration. Such an approach guarantees a low outlay, since if anything serious fails on the car it is discarded and another purchased. However, to avoid a succession of bad buys it is more critical than ever to use the information in this book to maximize the chances of getting a series of usable cars.

Buy a wreck, build for years

The alternative involves paying less for a poor or incomplete car, then buying parts as you build the vehicle yourself or pay a workshop to do so. This approach allows you to pause if finances run low but the final value will be less than your outlay, and it's worth considering whether paying more initially might not be better and more fun overall.

Servicing

Job	Interval
Basic oil change	3000 miles
Annual service	6000 miles or 12 months
Major service	18,000 miles or 3 yearly
Adjust valve clearances	24,000 miles or 4 yearly
Other?	As needed

Modern traffic holds no fears.

XJ Series parts prices (approximate)

Mechanical parts

Brake pads Front ●13/rear ●10
Disc Front ●55pr/rear ●41pr
Brake master cylinder ●63
Brake servo ●155
Head gasket set ●48
Gearbox rebuild ●950
Differential rebuild ●500
Fuel pump ●50-75 (depends on fuel injection or carb)
Exhaust (stainless) ●400
Radiator ●200
Clutch kit (plate, housing and release bearing) ●135
Alternator ●120 (depends on model)
Water pump ●80
Shock absorbers ●22 per shock front or rear (x6)
Wiper motor ●70
Fan motor ●80
Thermostatic switch ●15
Carburettor rebuild kit ●40 each
Starter motor ●105

Bodywork

Door skin ●45
Windscreen ●100
Front wing ●168
Rear wing ●150
Bumpers – multi part, depends on model ●300
Rear light cluster ●70

Bare-metal re-spray, average ●3000
Fuel tank ●150

Trim

Complete trim kit ●1200
Dashboard top cover ●60
Front seat covers (pair) ●600
Rear seat cover ●600
Carpet set (wool) ●240
Door panels (excluding pockets) set 4 ●340
Covering kit for 4 armrests and pockets ●50
Covering kit for 4 door cappings ●25
Covering kit for 4 door handle escutcheons ●25
Rear parcel shelf (excluding vent) ●65
Centre console kit (vinyl) ●35
Headlining material ●80
Boot hardura kit (including side trims) ●115
Furflex kit ●80
Under-carpet soundproofing pads (set of 4) ●60

Used parts

Plentiful
Check literature for dealers
eBay carries some rubbish and some over-priced good items as well as some genuine bargains but remember to factor in shipping
Owner's club classifieds
Autojumbles/swapmeets

Good points

Good-looking and still a head-turner today

Models for most tastes and needs

A genuine classic in a world of pretenders

Superb engines and good transmissions

Great presence and fine view over the long bonnet

Smooth power and performance, with great refinement

Excellent ride and comfort, without soggy handling

Good steering and brakes for a big car

Very comfortable and luxurious interiors

Easily keeps pace with modern traffic

Full instrumentation and lots of extras if required

Excellent visibility in light, airy cabin

Good primary and secondary safety and strong body

User-serviceable, especially early cars

Makes driving a pleasure again

Civilised to drive and light controls, a car for both sexes

Excellent spares back-up

V12 at 80mph uses a gallon every 13 minutes!

Bad points

Rust prone – some more so, but none immune

Craig Talbot's year-round car.

Fuel consumption, especially large engines and automatics

Headroom for tall rear passengers, plus rear legroom in SWB

Headlining often sags

Braking effort higher than modern cars

Marginal wipers/washers by modern standards

Screen leaks, plus side window seals in coupés

Cost of V12 engine work and some specialist parts

Practical as well as pretty.

Complex suspension requires regular maintenance
Long rear overhang when parking
Security, for such a desirable car
Reliability of some original electrical connectors and parts
Overheating in traffic for poor cars in hot weather
Modest boot space for the luggage of 4-5 people

Summary
A superb and addictive road car, even today, dated only by fuel consumption and over-light controls on some models. To drive one is to love one. Not a cheap car to buy or run, but very rewarding. Requires regular maintenance and use to give of its best. Always likely to cost far more to restore than they sell for, but still worth it compared to running an anonymous modern second car.
The V12 can still keep ahead of many modern cars, and is supremely refined.
All are great mile eaters – luxurious enough to pamper, sporting enough to thrill.
Grace, space, pace indeed ...

4 Relative values
– which model for you?

Models

There are many Series XJ models, with a wide variety of prices to match. There are three Series, two wheelbases, three body types, and a total of four engines, with automatic and manual versions of many cars, meaning there's a model for most tastes. When it comes to choosing one, the priorities of a person merely wanting an XJ for gentle pottering on sunny days (for whom a 2.8 auto will serve well) are different from the person who wants to mix it over long distances with modern high-speed traffic, where a 4.2 or V12 is the best choice (the V12 S3 was not officially sold in the United States).

S1 cars look more 'classic', with their lower front bumper, taller grille and fussier detailing inside and out. S2 cars look more modern and sleek, despite similar dimensions, but have a reputation for poor build quality from the British Leyland era. They may have the furthest to climb, price-wise, however.

Ken Cantor's immaculate V12.

The limited number of XJC hardtop coupés means they will always be more rare and valuable, with the number of V12-engined models barely making it into 4 figures, and the number of V12 Daimler cars standing at only 407. The coupés were built using the short-wheelbase XJ floorpan, but needed heavy modification and manual construction to arrive at the unique cabin, door and wing structures.

'Final 100' V12s are the most valuable.

The S3 unveiled in 1979 is arguably the prettiest of them all, having benefited from deft Pininfarina styling touches to lighten the cabin and give it crisper cleaner lines, at the expense of a slightly taller look and only heavy long-wheelbase versions. The Bosch fuel injection first introduced on US-market late S2 cars was also used on V12 coupés and all 4.2/5.3 S3 cars. Jaguar ceased production of the 6-cylinder S3 XJ in 1987, although the S3 continued in V12 form until 1992 when the XJ40 shell was modified to accept the V12.

Jaguar did not use the Daimler name in North America in modern times, so the

Vanden Plas brand was used to denote the top of the range models, which featured boxwood inlaid veneers and full leather trim instead of a mixture of leather and vinyl.

Values

Due to the many models, engines, trim levels, etc., these are simplified and approximate values only. The dearest models are rated at 100% and others shown as a percentage of that value. Note, however, that the price you pay for a given model should depend more on condition than its notional value in this table. A 'final' batch of 100 Vanden Plas-badged V12s was made in 1992 and exported to Canada and these have a value somewhat above other Series 3 cars, though similar cars have turned up in Australia and elsewhere.

When new, automatic transmission cost extra and manual transmissions were generally regarded as entry level specification. Today, because of rarity, changing tastes and fuel economy benefits, manuals normally command a premium, especially in North America where, for most of XJ production, they were not available.

Similarly, Daimler cars which originally cost significantly more than Jaguars sometimes sell cheaper, due to their less sporting image than equivalent Jaguars. Sometimes, however, a good Daimler with all the trimmings still sells for more. All values will vary by condition and market.

S2 V12 Daimler/Jaguar coupés	100%
S2 6-cyl Daimler/Jaguar coupés	85%
S1 Daimler Double Six VDP	85%
S3 Daimler Double Six VDP*	85%
S1 XJ6 4.2	75%
S1 XJ12	75%
S2 Daimler VDP 4.2	70%
S1 Daimler Double Six	65%
S2 Jaguar/Daimler 4.2	65%
S3 XJ12 Sovereign	65%
S2 XJ12	60%
S3 XJ12	60%
S3 XJ6 4.2	55%
S1 Jaguar/Daimler 2.8	50%
S2 XJ6 3.4	50%
S3 XJ6 3.4	45%

Rare doesn't mean expensive, if in poor condition.

* The final batch of cars are probably valued at 85% if you can find one, or, in exceptional cases, even more.

Unlike some exotic Jaguars, Series XJ cars are plentiful and mostly well used. The potential for wasted time chasing after poor examples is, therefore, great, although on the plus side you are unlikely to have to travel very far to examine at least some cars and get a feel for what you need to check. Because they are still nice cars even when worn out, sellers may overclaim and paint too good a picture, especially in advertisements, so be sure to call first to eliminate poor examples.

Ask specific questions. For example, instead of simply asking if the body is good, ask is there rust on the doors; is there rust around the screens; is there rust in the sills, etc.? It is less easy for sellers to misleadingly answer direct questions. Try to assess the credibility and attitude of sellers, and decide if you're comfortable buying from them.

Ask specific questions about rust-prone areas.

Where is the car?

Unless you are looking for a rare model, such as a coupé or an S1 Vanden Plas, you will probably do better seeing a larger number of cars reasonably close by, than travelling long distances and viewing fewer examples. Often, cars from areas where salt is used on the roads, or from coastal areas, suffer more corrosion than inland or salt-free cars. Exact specifications varied, sometimes significantly, according to market – so for

Ask about non-standard fitments.

fewest inspection/compliance issues buy from your own market.

Dealer or private sale?

As with most Jaguars, some of the biggest XJ risks concern bodywork and structural rust, although for fuel-injected cars – especially V12s – mechanical and electrical complexity can also pose significant buying risks. A good dealer should only select solid cars for resale, but it is also true that dealers may have better facilities for hiding body problems convincingly than an amateur with filler and aerosol cans. In general, the more you pay the better the car – especially from

Try to view at the seller's home or premises.

long-established Jaguar specialists with reputations to protect. There is nothing wrong with asking how they would deal with any problems that might occur and whether they offer their own warranty as standard, or can arrange a third-party warranty which gives good cover. Dealers usually also offer finance, which is another good reason for using them if you want to buy a higher-priced car.

Dealers buy and sell through trade auctions, and you can do the same, where usually a 24 hour warranty is supplied (see Chapter 10). For the very cheapest cars, private sales are normally best – especially from long-term owners or fellow enthusiasts who have looked after the car with pride. If you're happy to risk major work or want a total Do-It-Yourself project, *Classic Car* small ads or eBay are other sources.

When phoning an advertiser, simply ask about 'the car', to see if they are selling more than one. This does not guarantee they are a trader but it's a strong indication. Once you have discussed the car, ask how long they have owned it and what papers they have. Good ownership involves significant maintenance, so they should have either receipts for parts if they have done work themselves, or bills from a service shop. Dealers may know less about a car but should have some documentation.

Condition (body/chassis/interior/mechanicals)
Query the car's condition in as specific terms as possible – preferably citing the checklist items described in Chapter 9.

Viewing arrangements
It's always preferable to view at the vendor's home or business, not at the roadside or a carpark. A private seller's name and address should be on the car's documents, so beware stories about the documents being re-issued or their name left off on purpose to minimise the number of previous owners, since a car might go through several uncaring owners that way. Have at least one viewing in daylight and preferably dry weather to check the paint and body properly. If you are forced to view in wet weather use the opportunity to check for screen leak dampness or wet floors.

Reason for sale
Genuine sellers will explain why they are selling and, since XJs are all big thirsty cars, it may just be because the seller has run out of money. More sinister would be because they have just put the car in for an inspection and found lots of expensive

problems. Thankfully, nowadays many authorities, such as VOSA in the UK, permit on-line viewing of the reasons for failure, as well as the advisory notices issued at the last test, even if the car passed. Almost as bad is the owner who simply wishes to cut their losses and do the minimum to get the car ready or sale to recoup their outlay. Either way, you can inherit the bills they avoided.

LHD/RHD conversions

XJ cars sold widely in most markets, so apart from the occasional historic or dry state American car repatriated to Japan, UK or Australasia, there is little demand for LHD/RHD conversions. If you are contemplating buying or importing one, remember it's not just the steering wheel and dashboard which need changing but also headlamps, wiper parking, and often the side lamp colours and speedometer type. Many American-spec cars used large ugly rubber bumpers and these are not as easy to switch for the slimmer European parts as it may appear. North American cars also often used lower compression, catalysts, air injection, charcoal vapour canisters and other emissions-related equipment, and also had extra side repeater lights which spoil the clean lines and can be a source of rust around the mounting holes.

Originality

Total originality almost always boosts value, apart, perhaps, from cars which have had later additions, such as air pumps or catalysts and rubber bumpers removed. They were fitted for good reason, however, so check your regulators can accept slightly reduced safety or emissions standards.

'Lumped' cars with non-Jaguar engines are worth even less except to a very small segment of the market which prefers the use of an American V8. Very occasionally, a much later Jaguar engine and transmission may be installed, such as from a manual 6-cylinder XJ-S, for example. These all-Jaguar conversions, if done well, benefit from better performance and economy/refinement than the originals, but again the market is smaller.

Matching data/legal ownership

Early XJ cars have chassis, body, engine and gearbox numbers on old-style ID alloy plates, whilst later ones used a single long VIN number. All the numbers on the major parts

Ask if numbers match the documents.

and data plate should match to justify a top price, although changed engines, etc. noted on registration documents are acceptable, especially if the original parts come with the car.

Does the vendor own the car outright, or is money owed on it or is it even stolen? Finance checks can often also confirm if the car has ever been a write-off. In the UK the following organisations supply vehicle data:

DVSA – 0300 123 9000
HPI – 0845 300 8905

AA – 0344 209 0754
DVLA – 0844 306 9203
RAC – 0800 015 6000
Other countries will have similar organisations.

Roadworthiness

Does the car have a roadworthiness or emissions certificate (an MoT certificate in the UK, which can be verified on 0300 123 9000 or gov.uk/check-mot-status)? Similar checks are available in some other markets. Californian smog-related fittings are generally not required for roadworthiness in other markets and even many American states will pass a car without the air pump and exhaust gas recirculation equipment or carbon canisters.

Unleaded fuel

All XK and V12-engined cars have valve seats suited to unleaded fuel, although depending on local specifications it may be necessary to retard the ignition a fraction on low-octane fuel.

Payment

A cheque/check will take several days to clear and the seller may prefer to sell to a cash buyer. Cash can also be a valuable bargaining tool, but a banker's draft or money order may be acceptable so ask beforehand.

Buying at auction?

See Chapter 10.

Professional vehicle check

Series XJs are heavy, complicated and fast cars compared to simpler classics. Therefore, some important checks need to be made before running one in modern traffic. Your local motoring organisation or marque/model specialist will usually conduct a professional examination for a fee. For V12s, try to perform, or pay for, a full compression check. One or two poor cylinders can be missed, even on road test, if you are unfamiliar with V12s.

Other organisations providing car checks in the UK are:
AA – 0800 056 8040 (motoring organisation with vehicle inspectors)
RAC – 0330 159 0720 (motoring organisation with vehicle inspectors))
Other countries will have similar organisations.

6 Inspection equipment
– these items will really help

The most important inspection tool is your eyes, so be sure to bring a good torch and inspect the car at least once in daylight or excellent artificial light. When checking interiors or the hoses and pumps in the boot, your nose will also help detect existing or recently-removed damp and mold, as well as fuel seepage. Running your fingers over hidden seams or paintwork can detect rust, poorly re-welded flanges, and botched filler patches respectively, by touch. As for conventional tools, besides the torch you will benefit from taking with you:

This book
A magnet (not too strong) to check for filler
One, or ideally two, trolley jacks to give safe access
Small mirror on a stick for inaccessible areas
Spark tester/inductive timing light and/or spare plug
Probe (a small screwdriver works very well)
Digital camera
A knowledgeable friend

Useful extras

Hand tools are also important for inspection.

Compression gauge with long connector (especially for V12s), antifreeze concentration hygrometer, test strips for checking combustion products in coolant (head gasket leak), IR thermometer for checking misfiring cylinders.

There are fibreglass wings and other XJ panels available and, although these can generally be easily spotted, a magnet is conclusive proof. It also helps for checking door bottoms, sills, wheelarches and valences. A special tool for checking paint thickness is useful though not cost-effective for occasional use.

The camera is handy for photographing interiors or external rust areas to get feedback later on what is probably needed for repair. Remember that visible corrosion is always far less than hidden rust. For example, some bubbling or staining where the sill joins the rear wheelarch may look minor, but may mean this entire structural area has rotted from the inside because of water leaking down inside from the rear screen.

A small screwdriver can be used – with care – as a probe, particularly on the inner and outer sills, chassis sections over the IRS where the mounts attach, and front chassis legs ahead of the subframe (as well as the subframe itself). The sill closing panels inside the wheelarches front and rear should also be solid, and can be probed hard since there is no gloss paint here. The rear lower quarters and both valences are often rotten and can be probed hard if they look suspect, since any marks will not be visible. They are not structural, however. Radius arm mounts and floors, inner sills, boot floor, and anywhere else that looks rusty or filled should be probed.

The stick mirror helps check the underside, around the manifolds if the exhaust

is blowing, or for seepage from a coolant or fuel joint on the inlet side, or around the IRS cage if the handbrake seems weak or there is dampness from differential oil or brake fluid seepage. A full on-ramp inspection is obviously ideal, but two trolley jacks plus appropriate axle stands can make a lot of viewing room, either along one side at a time or one end at a time.

A dark or shady spot will help you spot any high tension arcing around the distributor, coil or plug wires. To tell if a V12 is running on all cylinders it's good to bring a small in-line or other spark tester or spare plug to use on each plug lead in turn. Not all plugs are equally easy to reach, especially if emissions equipment is fitted, but it's still worth checking because engines can sometimes run for prolonged periods making seemingly good power with one or more 'dead' cylinders and expensive damage. Some electronic ignitions are damaged by running with a plug lead detached and no plug. An inductive timing light saves disconnecting any plug wires and can be used to check the distributor is advancing properly if the vacuum connections are disconnected and plugged.

If possible, use a test strip to check for the right type and strength of coolant corrosion inhibitors, since neglect in this area – not unusual in frost-free climates – can ruin the internals of the 6-cylinder and, especially, all-alloy V12 engines. Ideally, you'll also be able to check for combustion gases in the coolant from a faulty head gasket. Both are useful back-ups for the normal visual check for bubbling while the engine is running and the smell of exhaust fumes in the coolant.

A compression tester is ideal for the most thorough engine check and accessibility on the sixes couldn't be easier. For the 5.3-litre engines with 12 plugs to remove and replace, it's not a trivial task, so you probably won't be able to do

that sort of work until either a final detailed inspection or you own the car, by which time you're stuck with the results either way. If there is a single test worth paying for in advance, however, it's probably this.

Road test

Tell the owner not to start the car before you arrive, so you can check how easily it starts from cold. The automatic enrichment devices on older cars can fail and various cold-start components on fuel-injection cars may also cause poor starting that only appears when cold. You also need to see the car start from cold to look for start-up

A full road test is important.

smoke. A brief puff of blue smoke on the first rev is acceptable, but thereafter the exhaust should be clear or merely clouded with rapidly-clearing water vapour. If in the driving seat, press the brake before start-up and check the pedal moves a little further when the engine starts, showing that the servo is working.

Once underway, the ride should impress you with its soft but controlled movement that irons out bumps and gives an old-fashioned 'magic carpet' ride compared to modern cars with low profile tyres. Listen for knocks or clunks and whining or moaning noises in hubs/suspension and driveline. An XJ6 should be smooth, and anything that feels or sounds like looseness or clonking indicates work is needed – ranging from a loose wheel bearing, worn ball joint, rubber bushes or mounts, to a differential slack in its cage, or a damaged universal joint. Elsewhere, tailpipes can rattle where they emerge from the rear valance, either always or only when the car is cold or going over bumps. This loud noise from the back is relatively easy to differentiate from noises in the driveline and may clear up once the engine gets warm and the exhaust moves around.

Manual or automatic, the car should accelerate cleanly and briskly/strongly/very strongly, depending on engine size. There should be no smoke under acceleration once fully warm, or on the overrun, when puffs of blue smoke in the mirror indicate worn guide seals or rings. An exception is a V12 (especially HE version) that has been habitually driven slowly. These can smoke alarmingly for some minutes when first driven at high revs in a low gear, but it should clear up and then not recur during the drive. Any car that struggles up hills or when overtaking slower vehicles probably needs a tune-up at least, or a rebuild at worst.

The brakes should be able to lock all four wheels on a dry straight road under hard braking, albeit with higher pedal pressure than required with modern cars. Juddering normally indicates warped or corroded discs and/or suspension problems, although it can just be pad deposits on the discs from holding brakes on after a hard stop. The XJ has front anti-dive geometry but the car still dips in a firm stop. Bottoming out probably hints at tired springs or shock absorbers, which can be confirmed with a static ride height check or the 'corner bounce' test respectively. Make several low speed full-lock turns to check for wheel rubbing or power steering noises. V12s or others fitted with a Powr-Lok limited slip differential may creak a little at full lock from the rear axle especially without correct LSD oil. Check that the handbrake works and releases fully, especially if the car has remained unused for some time. It should hold the car on a hill, although the under-dash handle may need a good pull. Check that the dash brake warning light operates, although they tend to be dim – leading to many people forgetting to release the brake. This results in pads wearing down to metal or breaking up.

The sixes are smooth, and swift in the larger sizes, but if you are not used to the power and smoothness of the V12, an apparently well-performing car may actually be misfiring or conceal other substantial faults. The V12 engine is extremely durable and can easily last 200,000 miles but needs proper oil and coolant changes and must not be allowed to overheat. Try an envelope or loosely folded paper behind the tailpipe while the warm car is idling. This will amplify the noise of any 'off-beat' rhythm and point to low speed misfires, although few engines idle perfectly. Do not worry about low idle oil pressure when hot, especially on twelves, provided it climbs as soon as the revs move off idle. The manual gearboxes should be silent except in reverse sometimes. The auto boxes should change almost imperceptibly and you may never feel the first to second change during the whole test.

Watch the temperature gauge on all cars, but especially V12s, as overheating is dangerous – up to 90°C is normal. An XJ road test is much like any other but you will have to try harder to sense noises or other problems because the car is better insulated from road and engine noises than most classics. There should be little or no wind noise up to quite high speeds. Marked differences side to side (assuming all windows and doors are fully closed and seals present) are probably due to upper door fit which can be 'adjusted' with a large lever once you own the car.

Minor and electrical controls should work, although the washers and wipers, for example, cannot match more powerful modern items. Many heat and ventilation controls are actuated by vacuum, so you'll probably hear a soft movement of air and a faint tap or clonk as the flaps move, shortly after the controls are adjusted. Central locking and window switches may result in sluggish or absent movement, but often this is through lack of use. Typically, the driver's window generally works best, the front passenger's next, and the rear ones may move hardly at all. The rocker switches are generally cleanable inside, and the circuits are thermally-protected so any problems are usually not too serious.

If all seems well and you make it back to base without drama you're ready to progress. When the engine and transmission are fully warm, move the auto gear selector through all positions 2-3 times and leave the engine idling while you pull the dipstick and clean/re-insert to check the fluid level is correct for the hot markings. If the fluid is brown instead of red, or smells burnt, this shows lack of maintenance. If standing by the car, listen for engine clatter from the timing chain or top end on start-up. Paradoxically, a near silent engine with no valve noise indicates clearances

Leapers are incorrect on Daimlers!

may have closed up and risk burning a valve. A really loud tapping, especially from the exhaust side on a fuel-injected engine suggests a possible loose tappet guide which is expensive and urgent to repair. Correct valve noise is a light 'rustle'.

Under the bonnet the shuddering of a cold engine can cause airboxes or other components to rattle and clonk against the inner wings or the diagonal struts or other points, although they too may be silent when the engine is smoother and warm. Listen for blowing from the manifolds where they fix to the downpipes or the head. The four studs per manifold outlet are often incomplete or loose if the exhaust has struck an object, or corners of the manifolds have snapped off or vibrated slack. On V12s, exhaust leaks are more problematic due to accessibility issues.

Concours contender

XJs do not command the high prices of the rarer models, such as E-types. There is, therefore, less incentive for spending large sums on total restoration which would cost far more than the car is worth. The best cars are, consequently, often immaculately looked-after originals rather than chequebook restorations. This is good in terms of originality, but in some cases means that if you do not keep up the same high standards, or run the car year round, they can deteriorate far more quickly than cars that have been stripped back to bare metal and repaired in all the vulnerable spots before painting or rust-proofing with modern materials.

With a supposed 'concours' car you ought to be able to take many aspects for granted pending more detailed checks later. Assuming the major components are standard, you will need an expert to help you check the detail points if you care about them. Knowing how 'correct' a car is needs experience, but buying a car with successful concours history should mean you are buying a good specimen.

Body and interior

Is the correct hard, shiny steering wheel

Early 2.8 Daimler. Note reversing light reflectors.

If it looks this good, it probably *is* good.

fitted with the chrome horn ring for S1, rubber centre pad for S2, and leather for S3 only, with two horn thumb buttons on the last Series 3 cars? Are the instruments chrome ringed for early S1, black with silver edge for S2, and all black for S3 – recessed for the later cars? Is the dash top clean and uncracked, and the veneer unmarked, with the under-dash panels, wiring and glovebox linings all clean and in place? Have the legends or trim paint worn off the central switches? Is the rev counter red-lined correctly for the engine fitted (6500rpm is only for V12s)? Is the radio a period item, and are the original style door speakers fitted? Is the interior trim held with invisible clips or incorrect visible screws? Do the mirror controls work if fitted? Are the wheels the correct pressed steel with chromed embellisher and hub caps (S1 and S2, two different styles). Chromed steel wheels were used on the higher spec cars and Kent or Pepperpot/Ogle alloys for S3 and V12 cars. Are 'Growler' badges used or D for Daimler? Wire wheels were not standard fitment on any Series XJ, nor were leaper bonnet ornaments, although many cars may have been fitted with both, especially by American dealerships. Is the exhaust correct, with the straight pipes on early S1, followed by chromed swan necks on S1 and 2 and rolled-edge trims only on S3?

Are boot boards and boot lining trim correct? Is the toolkit present, with a bagged cantilever jack and wheel brace? Are the twin SU pumps and pipework correct for early cars, with switchover valves and a high pressure pump for the fuel-injected versions?

Are panel gaps good, with no door drop – especially on the driver's door and on coupés? Do all the openings close properly? Are there any rust signs around the screens or traces of water damage inside? Typical headlining drop should have been repaired in top quality cars, and the seat leather should be supple with no loose stitching or torn and stained door cards or loose trim, especially arm rests and console lids.

Daily driver

The fifteen minute checks for a moderately-priced car should concentrate on the fundamentals, especially when buying privately. Only buy a car from an individual who can prove that they are the person named in the car's registration document (V5C in the UK) and, preferably, at the address shown in the document. Also check that the VIN or chassis number and engine numbers of the car match the numbers in the registration document. On American cars a VIN number tag is visible through the windscreen, and the engine number at the rear of the block is also stamped on the ID plate riveted to the inner wing and sometimes a sticker on the door return panel. American cars used twin 1.75" Strombergs. Elsewhere, the earliest XJ6 cars used two

Lift carpets on all cars to check floors.

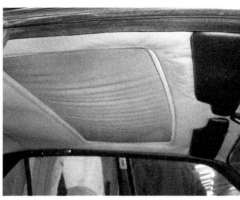

Many headliners drop more than this.

HD8 SU carbs, which were later changed to HS8s and then HIFs with integral float chamber. From S2, carburettor cars also used a crossover induction system to blend hot air with cold so that the carburettors were fed at a constant 40°C.

All XJs came with power steering, so check for leaks and clean fluid.

Rough but complete

Because XJs are large, fast, mass-produced cars from an earlier age when rust-proofing was crude at best, you must inspect the bodywork as closely as possible. This is the most expensive, time consuming, and skill-dependent aspect of the car to rectify if

Wheel removal makes inspection easy.

in poor condition. Even with a V12 it may be better to purchase a car with suspect mechanicals in a confirmed good body, than take on a structurally questionable XJ with good running gear.

Does the car sit right, with no corner lower than any other? Under the bonnet, does all look tidy and corrosion free? Does the bonnet hold itself open and look dent free from inside as well as outside, indicating that no filler has been used?

On the inside, is the trim in good condition and smell of leather, or mould indicating a water leak? Does it look neglected or cared for (as opposed to polished merely for sale)? Is the laminated screen clear or milky around the edges, and do the windows work and is the glass scratched, especially on the driver's side? Does the interior adjustable door mirror work, if fitted, and do all the electrics function, especially the wipers and airconditioning, if fitted?

Try to see as much of the underside as possible – ideally on a lift. The floor and chassis rails should be body colour over stonechip, normally with good underseal on top. Check sills for filler – especially in front of and behind the doors, where

No handbrake adjustment remaining.

Look at boot floor and valance area.

Split seals can fail inspection and admit water.

they meet the bulkheads. Same thing around the wheelarches and the vulnerable front and rear corners. The boot floor is prone to scraping and subsequent rusting and perforation from inside and out.

Pull the wheels to and fro hard at the top as a a preliminary check for slack bearings or worn suspension/drive universals or output bearings. Have someone turn the steering wheel to and fro while you feel/ view the tie rod ball joints for movement. Look at the tyres for unusual wear, indicating suspension or alignment problems. Look for split or crumbling suspension bushes at all pivots or attachment points. Check for leaks from the differential input and output seals, especially if oil is being lost near the rear discs. Oil mist around the differential breather is normal. Check the top, sides and front/back of the engine for leaks from the cam covers, head gaskets, core plugs or front or rear crank seals respectively. Oil leaking from the bellhousing can also be gearbox oil, but the smell is noticeably different and, in both cases, the engine has to come out for a repair.

Basket cases

Some XJs – especially the rarer models – are sold as 'barn finds' awaiting restoration. They can seem cheap but normally are not as good a buy as a better car needing less work. If low price is your main criterion, and you can wait a long time to finish the project, basket case cars may be worth a look.

Even existing repairs to bodywork may be suspect. Try to assess the repair competence of the seller if it was DIY work. Do you trust them to have cut back the rot aggressively enough, or did they opt to patch onto questionable metal?

Finally, take note of the data plate and cross check against the seller's documents.

8 Key points

– where to look for problems

Key aspects to check on Series XJs are:

Structural bodywork
Cosmetic bodywork and seals
Engine condition
Transmission, suspension and brakes
Instruments and electrics
Interior trim

Bodywork

The XJ cars are all of monocoque (frameless) construction so most of the common rust areas affect the integrity of the structure, directly or indirectly. Although rust-proofing improved on later cars, even those are by now often seriously

Low-budget repairs are rarely perfect.

corroded, so a thorough appraisal is vital. Even if a car has been restored you need to check the type and extent of corrosion and assume there will be some hidden rust – even from condensation in box sections. A recent coat of paint can hide a lot of problems which will erupt later. Fewer of these cars will have had serious panel craft work done and are more likely to have been patch welded and polyester resin filled. It's impossible to know how the metal was prepared before covering with filler and paint, and amateur paint jobs may involve long periods without topcoat, leading to microblistering or corrosion.

Brightwork

The XJ cars mostly have high quality chrome-plate or stainless exterior trim. If it looks OK it's probably fine, although the trim around the screens, or more accurately the rubber seals in which they sit, can give trouble and allow water to collect and leak. Rust around the base of the front or rear screen is consequently very common, and is both unsightly and tricky to repair. Because the screens need to come out to repair this, owners often postpone remedial work but, unfortunately, if water leaks

At least the common rust spots are obvious.

in it normally trickles down the body pressings to puddle lower down. From there it can quietly rust the floorpan or under the rear seats. More damagingly, it often ruins the critical corners where the sills meet the stiffening body sections in front of the rear wheelarches or the front of the doors. Rotting from the inside out means that by the time you see bubbling it's too late for a simple fix.

Other common rust traps are the rear quarters under the petrol tanks, the tanks themselves, the front and rear valances, the transverse seam between rear valance and boot floor, the headlamp surrounds, rear lower sections of the front wings, the door bottoms, bonnet hinge areas and boot lid.

Engines

All Jaguar engines are inherently durable, but overheating or other neglect can cause problems. For the V12s there is no substitute for a compression test – which is tricky enough on pre-HE engines and even more difficult via later HE plug locations. All cylinders should be within about 10% of each other to avoid expensive trouble.

Mild oil leaks from cam covers, etc., are common but heavy losses require investigations. There should be no coolant leaks or white powdery deposits from former seepage.

Transmission

The transmissions are dependable and are more likely to be damaged from neglect than wear, so check for excessive whine or knocks – especially on hard acceleration – harsh shifting, slipping clutches or to/fro clunking. Most parts for the entire powertrain are long-lasting and readily available. The strong differential is normally good for further work after new seals.

Suspension and brakes

The front and rear suspension dampers and rubber components wear eventually, as do the metal pivots, especially if not greased routinely. Apart from track rod ends and front wheel bearings, most need some expertise to fix. Brakes – especially the difficult to service rear discs – are often worn, which is bad news on such rapid heavy cars. The difficulty of working on them means you probably need to budget for professional refurbishment, although with good tools and care, it is all repairable by the home mechanic.

Electrics

6-cylinder XJ electrics are basic and computer-free up to the end of Series 2 cars and on carburetted Series 3 cars. Apart from the Series 1 and earliest Series 2 V12s, the 5.3-litre cars all had fuel-injection and electronic ignition. Most problems are due to loose connections, dirty switch contacts or broken individual components which are normally easy to troubleshoot. Check the full range of controls and gadgets for operation, but do not be surprised if the driver's window works better than the front passenger's (and both work better than the rear windows which are much less often used). On fuel-injection cars, check the engine harness wiring for brittleness and cracks.

Interiors

The interior of an XJ is normally a mixture of man-made and natural materials, and their survival depends on how they have been treated. Most are easy to inspect visually but all are expensive to repair, either in material or labour costs, or both. Dropped headlining or warped door cards, loose armrests, split seat seams, cracked or lifted veneer, torn or holed carpet and split vinyl are all common after 30-40 years. Check for musty smells from water leaks and sickly sweet smells from leaked coolant or hydraulic fluids.

9 Serious evaluation

– 60 minutes for years of enjoyment

Circle Excellent, Good, Average or Poor boxes for each check and add up points at the end. Be realistic, and especially vigilant where bodywork is concerned, and with regard to engine checks on the V12.

Overall stance

An XJ6 should sit flat and level front-to-back and side-to-side, or very slightly higher at the rear, especially with low fuel load. If sagged to one side – typically the driver's side – or drooping at the back, the springs are tired. On level ground the bottom of the front subframe should be about 6⅜in above ground with most 215 width tyres and 6¼in with 205s.

Eric Féron's US coupé stands well.

Body panels

A good XJ should have undistorted panels with even shut lines, and the doors should follow the body contours and not stick out at the corners. Look for filler bulges along the bottom of doors or wings and around the headlamps, arches and sills. Feel the wheelarch returns for rough metal, or double thickness or seams from repairs. Mud-filled seams on sill ends or arches, or around the headlights or lower wing fronts can hide rot, so clean and inspect by torchlight. Front and rear valances suffer badly, and the lower radiator crossmember (visible through the grille) is structural.

Stand back to look at reflections and panel gaps.

Underside and sills

Beware heavy gobs of underseal over poor welding or rusted metal. The fronts of the footwells suffer, as do the sill seams, front and rear jacking points, and the radius arm attachment points. The rear lower quarter-panels around the tanks are often rotten but are detachable. Check for rust in the chassis rails within about a foot of the rear suspension cage mounts, and if the rear screen appears rusty be especially suspicious of rust in the lower rear sill area where the wheelarch joins, as water collects here. If possible, look under the seat cushion for water/rust from a leaky rear screen. The front upper section of the sills is hidden behind the wings, but look from inside the rear edge, past the open door, and check for clues of corrosion, such as packed mud or bubbling at the rear lower edge of the wings.

Sills should be solid rather than patched.

Bonnet and inner wings

The hinge attachment points rust from inside the box section and this affects shut lines and bonnet closure. There will be tell-tale marks where the bonnet has hit the top of the wings if it has closed crookedly in the past. Typically, the left-side hinge

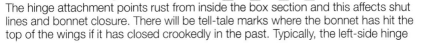

area is worst affected where it takes the strain of the bonnet prop mechanism. Inner headlights don't rust as badly as the outer wings. Inner wings should be free of corrosion at the front bottom corner where they meet the chassis rails (under the washer bottle especially, where it tends to stay damp) and along the top edge where the wings attach. Chassis rails should be undamaged and not creased or patched from an accident. Top shock absorber mounts can be checked, as can the battery tray area.

Bonnets rot and distort around hinge.

Boot lid

Rust strikes from inside, either through seal leakage, condensation, or leakage via holes from missing or poorly-fitted badges. Higher-spec models have a one-piece lid liner, whereas others use stick-on panels between the reinforcement stiffeners. The lower edge should not strike the body, and the shut lines should be even all around.

Check for good lower boot edge.

Floors

The carpets and underlay must be lifted to check the inner sill to floor seams, rear bulkhead seams, and front footwells. Check seat and safety belt attachments points. The foam strips in the channels are great sponges so press them to feel for dampness which may mean the car was dried out in a hurry for your inspection.

Floors and inner sills are structural.

Doors

Check door gaps and feel along the bottom edges – even re-skinned doors may have bad frames. Coupé doors are especially vulnerable to knocks as they open so wide, and they are expensive to repair because good secondhand replacements are scarce. Use your eyes, hands and your bodywork probe to check door apertures for rust in the corners of the openings at the base of the A B and C pillars. Door drop is an issue for driver's doors, especially on the coupés. Doors should fit flush and close with a thud not a clang. Door cards should be flat and even, with undamaged armrests and pockets securely attached. Check that the front opening quarter-lights open and seal properly on S1 cars, and that any remote control mirrors and manual or electric windows and central locking work. Door perimeter seals should be intact, and can be checked for fit by closing the door onto a sheet of paper in various positions.

Typical bottom edge corrosion.

Petrol tanks and pipework

The petrol tanks frequently rust from underneath, and the pipes running into the boot space corrode. Look for signs of leakage or lifted paintwork below the car.

This pipe leaks fuel onto the exhaust!

Inside the boot, remove the spare and undo the fuel pump cover to check for correct anti-vibration-mounted fuel pumps and leak-free feeds and returns (fuel-injected cars). Wiring should be clamped firm, not hanging loose, and well insulated rather than cracked or with bare strands showing. The fuel filter towards the front on the right should be solidly mounted too, with no signs of weeping, chaffed pipework, or heavy fuel smells. While the fuel pump cover is off check the electric aerial motor, drain and relay on early cars. Check also the welded seam between the rear valance and boot floor, as this can split.

Vinyl roof/sunroof/convertibles

Many Daimlers and Vanden Plas models of the seventies came with a vinyl roof, and a small number were made into two- or four-door convertibles by firms such as Lynx and Avon. In all cases check for tears or splits or separated seams and other damage. Converted soft tops use either a large fold-down hood or a roll-down landau-type top with door and window frames left intact. A Webasto-type folding sunroof should be checked for seal and tension, and metal reinforcing rods protruding through the sides. Electric sunroof checks include the seal around the hatch and good drains – as well as proper functioning. Factory sunroofs from this era only have a sliding action, no tilt.

Vinyl splits and admits water.

Paint

Various types of paint were used over the years. Thermoplastic paints were troublesome in hot climates. Because XJs are nowhere near as valuable as E-types or similar, there is less incentive to pay for a top class paint job. Many are, therefore, patched and blown over, or given a poor full spray job. This can be forgiven on a daily driver, but in a supposedly restored car it affects how long you could expect to use and enjoy it before problems re-appear. Check for overspray inside wheelarches or on rubber aperture seals and rubber cable sheaths into doors. Look for poor work inside the fuel filler recesses, along the tops of the inner wings where the outer panels bolt on, and under the front and rear bumpers. See also Chapter 14.

Some paint problems are extreme.

Lights & body trim

Non US markets used 7in outer lights and 5¾in inner lights always, whereas American cars eventually switched to four 5¾in lights, with wider trim rings to fill the gap, which look odd. Lucas lamps can gather condensation which blackens the plating of the bulb shield making the lights appear dark. Original S1 rear bumpers were one-piece, enclosing the numberplate lamps, and are expensive to replace, so check these parts carefully (many are still serviceable, at least for a daily driver).

Extreme neglect of lights and trim.

On S2 cars the rear bumper is a three-piece unit and easier to fix if only one part is bad. S3 cars and some US market S2 cars used rubber impact bumpers with separate chrome top trims, which are open underneath and tend to rust from the inside out. Chrome swage line trims were used on Daimler/VDP models and some Sovereigns. The headlamp trims, rear lights and most other moulded brightwork are 'pot metal' or Mazac, and, whilst they don't rust, they can oxidise and become pitted, which is not easy to repair. The stainless or deep chrome window frames usually survive well, and front side/indicator lights on S2 cars are all plastic, so the chrome doesn't rust but can dull or crack. The very earliest S1 cars used reversing lights with built-in red reflectors, but other cars have plain clear lenses and many have poor gaskets (which should be glued to the lamp body) that can let water into the boot lid to rot it from inside.

Original Lucas fog lights on top-of-the-range cars are both highly efficient and practical in fog, and valuable period accessories.

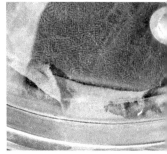

Leaks lead to trim damage.

Body seals

XJ refinement is largely due to effective sealing. Rubber seals around the front doors can come apart at the bottom front corner, or be worn or torn in other places. Furflex aperture trim is largely decorative but, if falling off the cant rail or vertical sections it can let in noise and looks unsightly. The top of the front bumper should have a flat rubber strip filling the gap between chrome and grille, and the transverse front scuttle seam just ahead of the wipers has a rubber noise/water seal right across the car. The front wheelarch filler panels have similar edge seals which need to be in good condition to prevent corrosion of the front sill and wings, but these are hard to check. Screen seals are critical (see later). Boot seals are generally fine, although water can get past via splits or accumulated debris, or bad fit following a repair.

Window channel felt glass seals should be snug to avoid wind whistle or window rattle. The horizontal external window wiper seals and felt internal strips should be supple to prevent scratching the window when raised or lowered. Coupés have unique seals around the frameless door and rear window glass, and these were marginal when new, and hard to find now.

Wheels and tyres

All Series XJ wheels are 15in steel or alloy. Wire wheels are aftermarket bolt-ons, or occasionally splined with hubs from another Jaguar. Check by tapping for loose spokes and look for corrosion. Pressed steel wheels are a plain shape for S1, sculpted for a few of the very last S1s and the S2, and normally hidden behind full stainless trims on S3s. Kent alloys were first used in the mid-'70s on V12s and Ogle

alloys (known as 'pepperpots') in the mid-'80s. Original high-profile 205 or 215 section tyres give the best ride and speedometer accuracy and must be the correct rating for these heavy fast cars.

Exhaust

[4] [3] [2] [1]

Apart from the early S1 cars which used straight tailpipes, all XJ cars used twin exhausts with characteristic swanneck trims, and a fully-rolled edge on S3s. The system is large and expensive, especially on V12s, so check for condition and attachment. Check especially that the rear silencers don't knock the bodywork. The overaxle pipes get neglected because of access difficulties, so ensure these are as good as the rest of the system may appear. Manifold to downpipe joints can work loose, but since they mostly use large metal olives it's often enough merely to tighten any loose nuts to regain a seal. Because of limited access, V12 manifold leaks are hard to repair.

Rear boxes can rattle against body.

Glass and wipers

[4] [3] [2] [1]

Objects sliding around on the parcel shelf can detach the demister connections from the element on each side. The problem with front and rear screens on all series XJ cars is water ingress. Although the rusting appears at the base where water puddles, it enters at the top and flows down the sides to collect lower down. The cure is to remove the screen and aggressively restore/replace any corroded metal, and refit with plenty of rust preventive and mastic. Check coupé side windows in particular for scratches and correct operation.

Typical rear glass seal damage.

The twin wiper system was upgraded over the years but a lazy action and parking problems are common. Later S3 switchgear is more robust, and has an intermittent wipe, but the wipers and washers are from an earlier age, though generally adequate. Check for corrosion around wiper pivots. Headlamp wipers, where fitted, are fragile and many will have been dismantled or disabled.

Rear suspension & brakes

[4] [3] [2] [1]

A good inspection requires that the wheels be taken off, but never rely on a rusty jacking point alone; use axle stands. Jacking up by the body will show any dangerous cage mount separation. Check wheel bearings, and feel for grinding or play in the universal joints, which act as both driveshaft and suspension links. Grease nipples under the alloy hub carrier are often sheared off and cause neglect of the important fulcrum taper rollers, leading to wear and 'strange'

Rear discs are frequently neglected.

Check rear dampers for leak stains.

handling. Look for weeping dampers and differential. A slight 'whine' is acceptable, but serious noise is not. V12s had a limited slip differential as standard, and strange creaking from the rear on tight slow turns can mean additives are missing from the diff oil.

An approximate check of limited slip clutches is to raise only one wheel and leave the transmission in neutral. It should take around 50lb/ft to overcome the clutches but, in old examples, it's often fairly easy to turn the wheel, although at least some resistance should be felt. Note: any car with a limited slip differential should not be tested on a roller-type brake tester at inspection, as these test wheels individually and may damage an LSD. The handbrake cable should be lubricated and unfrayed, handbrake pads can be felt if you can't see them, and there should be no oil or grease on the rear discs, which themselves should be largely corrosion and ridge free.

It's difficult to check for play at the inner and outer fulcrum pivots or radius arms, but a tyre lever and some judicious prying will reveal serious play. Good signs are fresh grease on all nipples and signs of spattering on adjacent bodywork.

Front suspension, brakes & steering

☒ ☒ ☒ ☒

XJs had anti-dive geometry as part of a separate front subframe, with its own rubber mounts like the IRS. This subframe can rust badly around the spring towers or from inside on the lower regions and spring pans. Prod very hard all over it, as the scratches will not be seen and this is an important safety area. Check the chassis rails around the subframe mounts at the front, as this area is less protected by oil seepage and can corrode badly. The crossmember under the radiator is also structural. The long plush springs may hide a broken coil. Pivot bushes are easy to inspect for perishing or swelling, and play is easiest to check if the car is lowered onto spring pan supports so the suspension is in its normal orientation at mid-laden position. Dampers can be visually inspected for top or bottom mount break-up or fluid leakage, and you should bounce each corner to check for damper condition.

Check all ball joints for split gaiters and slack, and the anti-roll bar rubbers and drop links. Look for rack movement when the wheels are on the ground – the steering mounts become oily and soft, making steering feel vague. Look for oil leaks from the power steering gear, although a wet rack is often caused by engine leaks rather than steering leaks.

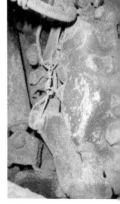

Check hoses and pads – 4 pots on S2 onwards.

Most XJs have vented front discs and 3 or 4 piston calipers. Check for signs of blued

Oil-softened front vee-mounts.

Solid if dented subframe – a critical part.

discs or worn pads from seizure, or cracked/weeping flex hoses or steel brake pipes. The servo should be clean and not heavily corroded, and the brake reservoir should have clean fluid with no sediment at the bottom or seepage from the rubber hoses or any other joint. Whilst under the car, inspect, by eye and by feel, the large bottom radiator hose and the radiator core itself from below.

Engine/gearbox mounts

The XJ has sandwich front engine mounts which can get covered in oil, especially on the right-side, and split or collapse. The rear gearbox mount is a steel coil spring sitting in rubber cups and surrounding a pin and rubber bush to control gearbox movement. The rubber bobbin is often split or missing, being awkward and messy, though not difficult or expensive, to replace.

Cabin trim

Even base model XJs have large, fully-trimmed cabins which are not cheap to refurbish. A musty smell means water leaks and a high suspicion of rust damage to floors (see elsewhere in this chapter). Dash tops and parcel shelves are vinyl that can split or crack from years of sun exposure and may show signs of water damage too. Centre consoles today often have holes or cuts in the trim or veneer where mobile phones have been installed, and these are unsightly.

Lacquer (not veneer) lifting around dials.

All cars used veneered dashboards, and many have lacquer problems, almost always starting at the edges where the laminate begins to peel from the backing wood around the glovebox opening or instrument holes. Original headliners normally show signs of bubbles or mould, requiring the front or rear screen to come out, which is inconvenient unless combined with a bare metal re-spray or window rust repair. Almost all seat facings were leather, although velour was an option, even on Daimlers, with the S2. Tweed-type cloth could be specified on S3s. Daimler and VDP door cards, centre consoles, armrests and seat sides were also leather, so replacement costs are higher.

Headrest foams on S2 cars have often collapsed. S3 headrests are slightly better, and the Daimler/ VDP headrests (including rear seats on S3) are usually better still. New covers and foams are available. Door cards often come loose or split due to water damage, and armrests can split or become detached if not properly re-fitted. Door pockets are lined with velour, which has often come loose, or the trim has split from outside the stool pocket. S1

A re-dye is easy. Repairing trim is not.

and many S3 cars used wooden door trim which suffers like the dashboard. Door treadplates were mostly aluminium, and these scratch more easily than stainless treadplates on late cars. Sun visors can split or collapse, and the under-dash panels may be hanging loose or missing. The inertia fuel cut off at the side of the dash should have a moulded plastic cover.

Carpets 4 3 2 1

Carpets lie above underlay backed with thick sound deadening plastic on later cars. The carpets are attached by plastic studs or Velcro. Underfelt and sound-deadening anti-drum material is used extensively and can trap liquids, so check for brake fluid leakage around the pedals or water from blocked AC drains or a leaking screen. Don't be fooled by new carpets. High-wear areas are vinyl, but inner sills are carpet-covered, and there is usually a lesser grade of carpet or 'Hardura' – a kind of vinyl/fibre trim panel, used in the boot and A-post areas.

Instruments & fuses 4 3 2 1

All XJs had six instruments and a clock. Rocker switches can malfunction if internal grease or corrosion have spoiled the contacts, but many are rebuildable and work fine after internal cleaning. Examine the general condition of the wiring and fuse panels – like all old cars the contacts for the fuses can get weak and corroded, as can the fuse caps themselves, so cleaning and attention to earth points often fix any inoperative electrical circuits. Note that American and European fuses operate on different load assumptions and are not strictly interchangeable for the same level of protection. Original fuses are best for the car.

Cooling system 4 3 2 1

This is one of the most critical areas if not serviced properly, or if filled with plain water instead of anti-corrosion coolant. The steel header tank corrodes if antifreeze is neglected, so check for pitting and leaks. Water level is difficult to check down the long neck on early cars, and can run low as a result. Hoses should be sound, with minimal corrosion at fittings. The top hose carries the hottest water and suffers first, but if replaced alone others may then fail due to age. Replacing a V12's many hoses is a major task that should appear in the service record – otherwise assume most if not all need renewing.

Jaguar's suggested leak sealant builds up and blocks radiator passages, as do rust and scale when plain water is used. Is the coolant clean and fresh-looking? Does the drain tap fitted

Check front of radiator through grille.

to the early radiators on the right work and run free? (It's best to ask the owner to demonstrate, rather than break something). Is the water pump pulley free of play and the belt tensioned correctly and in good condition?

With clean factory standard components the cooling system is fine, but a block full of rust and radiator full of scale means things are rarely in ideal condition today. Early cars had robust, 12-blade metal fans. Later plastic fans can show cracking

Check plastic fans for cracks.

at the base of the blades. Though not a common failure unless the centrifugal clutch seizes, any suspect fan needs to be replaced to avoid explosive damage. A cold fan should stop spinning after about half a turn if flicked round. Check that thermostatically-controlled fans work, especially on cars with air-conditioning.

Fuel system
Carburettors

US XJ6s used CD175 carbs. Others used SU HD8 (68-71), HS8 (71-75) or HIF (76-86). Strombergs were used on early V12s or some emissions control sixes. Various types of crossover, charge-warming and secondary manifold systems were used in order to improve emissions. S1 HD8 models used an electrical cold start enrichment device, later swapped for a bimetallic controlled device on S2 cars. Both starting devices can be unreliable and many are converted to manual choke. New units do work efficiently, however, so there's no reason for the car not to start instantly from cold, if all is well. Early V12s used 4 x Zenith Stromberg

HIF carburettors used to the end of production on 3.4s.

175 CDSE manual choke carburettors, and their issues are mostly split diaphragms, linkages out of sync, or loose connections. Carbs may also suffer sticking or binding pistons, or worn out float valves leading to flooding. SU float bowls should have narrow copper drains with fibre and alloy washers, but many will have snapped off so that water finds its way into the fuel. Throttle linkages and cables, and any manual choke mechanism should be free and smooth. Check that any cruise control fitments are properly attached, with no loose microswitch connections, split diaphragms or frayed cables. The single, boot-mounted fuel filter is often augmented by a filter near the engine and small ones to protect the pumps. When driving, the fuel tank changeover switch should also change the fuel gauge display and operate seamlessly. A totally empty tank may be hiding a leak from that side.

Injection

From the late 1970s, fuel injection was used on North American cars, before becoming universal on Series 3 4.2-litre engines, together with larger inlet valves. The 3.4-litre cars used carburettors throughout. A complete fuel injection check needs special equipment, but you can look for hardened rubber fuel hoses or signs of fuel weeping, which is normally most obvious on a cold engine

when cranking, before warm metal causes the fuel to evaporate and appear dry. Injector connectors should be unbroken and firmly held by spring clips, with the wires not split or cracked where they emerge, or indeed anywhere else in the engine harness, which becomes brittle with age, especially on the V12 cars.

Engine

Brief rattling on start up from cold is acceptable but, once warm, correctly adjusted Jaguar engines should run with just a light rustle from the valve gear. Loud tapping is at best a fiddly valve adjustment or at worst a loose tappet guide or piston. Look inside the oil filler cap to see if screws or plates have been fitted to clamp the tappet guides in place. Rumbles or clonks suggest bearing trouble.

Whirring from the timing chains is permissible, but metallic clatter is not. Screeching noises can indicate a loose belt or a worn pulley bearing, and the exhaust note should be regular and even at idle, although some hunting is common. All Jaguar engines are very

New core plugs. A good sign.

strong, however, and with clean oil and coolant – easily checked – should last many years. The early 2.8-litre engines had a reputation for burning pistons, but by now any problematic ones will have been fixed with better parts.

Obvious heavy dirt or loose-hanging wires, etc., spell lack of maintenance, but if the inside of the oil filler cap is clear of whitish 'mayonnaise' and there is no fuel smell on the dipstick or exhaust smell in the header tank, the engine is probably OK. There is no substitute for a full compression check, however, if engine condition is important and you don't wish to do a precautionary rebuild as part of a planned restoration. A wet/dry compression check is not trivial, especially on the 12s, but for such a complex and potentially expensive engine to refurbish, it's a wise investment of time and money and the equivalent of a house survey before purchase.

Once underway, audible pinging under load on a road test is a bad sign, though not that rare. It may not be easily remedied by retarding the timing, if due to weak mixture or unsuitably high compression for local fuel. The cylinder head(s) may have been skimmed to the point where a thicker head gasket is required to restore normal compression.

Transmission

Most XJs were automatics, with either the trusty Borg Warner or GM three-speed gearboxes. These give little trouble provided fluid is kept clean and topped up (See Chapter 7). Failure to take up drive immediately is a bad sign, especially if there is plenty of fluid. Some adjustments to brake bands, etc., are possible, but treat any transmission malfunction with suspicion. The selector lever can wear slightly (the bulb eventually fails too) and it may take some side-to-side wiggling to operate the reverse light switch, or an adjustment before kick-down operates properly.

Damaged transmission sump.

Manual gearboxes, with or without the Laycock Compact Type A overdrive, should operate smoothly and quietly, except for a whine in reverse, especially if the reverse gear components were not de-burred during any rebuild. The Series 3 manual was a very rare Rover-based 5-speed, and these are highly prized today, even if the all-synchro 4-speed Jaguar box plus overdrive effectively gives a similar spread of ratios. The overdrive should engage and disengage instantly by operation of the gearlever switch and can be checked by watching the rev counter as it's operated. There is, or should be, an interlock switch to prevent operation in reverse gear, which spells instant damage.

Ultra-rare S3 five speed.

The clutch on manual cars is heavy and long travel but not excessively so. It should engage and disengage quickly, smoothly and silently. The small reservoir near the brake servo may contain ugly dark fluid, and seals in the master or slave cylinder can leak, so check for fluid on the carpet or along the lines and beside the bellhousing. The clutch and brake and throttle pedals each have return springs but these are often broken so check for lazy or sloppy actions or loose carpet binding the movement.

Oil leaks and pressure

4 3 2 1

Apart from weeping below the rear crank seal, most leaks are easy to fix, so a very oily car has been neglected. The cam covers and rear cam feed connections can leak, as can the oil filter on Series 1 and 2 cars. The rear main bearing seal leaks more if the car has not been run for some time. V12s have a common leak from the timing cover inspection plug but should have no leaks from the front crank seal or timing chest or breather housing, though oil mist is normal. The oil return pipe to the sump from the filter block on sixes can

Oil from an engine, not steering, leak.

weep and a cracked sump or stripped drain plug on any engine (all too common) will require effort to repair, although drips may just be from a hardened or missing copper washer.

Oil pressure when cold may register 60-70psi briefly, but should settle to around 40psi when warm and running at around 2000rpm unless the relief valve is stuck. V12 engines are known for low idle oil pressure – sometimes below 10psi – but this is OK provided it climbs immediately when revved. Oil senders are notoriously inaccurate, however, and the actual gauge reading may also be affected by voltage stabilizer gremlins. Some Series 1 or 2 cars may have aftermarket spin-on filters, or the Series 3 XJ6 filter block fitted.

Distributor and ignition

All distributor rotors and bob-weights should be free and snap back under spring tension when released from the advance position. Unless you have documented evidence that a V12 distributor has been serviced recently you should assume it is seized and needs to be freed off urgently. There are reports of aftermarket distributor caps and rotor arms failing, although this may be partly due to fitting high power coils and electronic ignition (standard on V12s and Series 3 sixes, plus late Series 2 USA cars). Check any vacuum modules by observing baseplate movement when sucking on the vacuum tube, and check that the V12 distributor breathers are clear and routed correctly to avoid fuel vapours entering the distributor from a weeping

Later V12 S3 amplifier.

fuel connection and blowing up the distributor. HT leads should be clean and supple. The early finned OPUS amplifier is best sited away from engine heat but, if on or near the head check for brittle wiring. Also check the ballast resistor, if fitted, for cracking or burning and good connections. The coil, like the amplifier, is best located somewhere cool, but is often on top of the engine where it bakes.

Electrical

All XJs use a negative earth alternator system with battery gauge (voltmeter) to monitor charging and battery condition. The basic charging system is reliable, especially if a modern alternator with built in regulator is used. Check the overall wiring for tidiness and splits/bare connections, etc. Trouble spots include dirty relays for horns, fans, fuel pumps, and the large Hella headlamp relay. Depending on model, there is a range of additional thermostatic switches/sensors/relays, etc., and the only simple way to check is to operate every electrical system and check its functioning. Many problems are due to corroded fuses and fuse-holders, poor earths, damaged wiring and malfunctioning switches, most of which can be remedied easily with patience, a good wiring diagram and some small tools and contact cleaner.

Many cars had central locking and electric windows, which tend to suffer from lack of use rather than wear, so that often the driver's window works fine, the front passenger's not quite so well, and the rear windows are slow or stuck. They use thermal cut-outs so you'll need to wait for the circuit to be re-established if you hold the switches long enough for the trip to cut in. Lucas components are often ridiculed, but they generally last many decades, and it is age, or issues such as dirty connections or lack of care which cause trouble. From S2 onwards, electrical connections through the bulkheads were made by multi-pin plugs rather than harness wires passing through grommets. This is good when everything works well, but a source of mystery faults when things go wrong. The climate control system – with or without airconditioning – has a range of sensors of its own and these can also cause problems with dry joints or component breakdown and are occasionally somewhat inaccessible.

Evaluation procedure

Add up the points scored –
116 = first class, possibly concours; 97 = good/very good; 58 = average; 29 = poor.
Cars scoring over 97 should be completely useable and require the minimum of repair, although continued maintenance and care will be required. Cars scoring between 29 and 58 will require a full restoration – the cost of which will be much the same regardless of score. Cars scoring between 58 and 97 will need very careful assessment of the repair/restoration costs so as to decide a realistic purchase value.

10 Auctions
– sold! Another way to buy your dream

Apart from the S1 V12 Vanden Plas, or V12 Coupés, XJs are generally only rare if you are looking for a specific model, colour, or manual transmission. For the very best deals, however, or if you need to search for a rare car, you may wish to buy at auction.

Auction pros & cons
Pros:
Auctions are wholesale/trade markets and priced to suit. Auctions usually offer certified ownership, freedom from outstanding finance and a chance to check all paperwork and obtain a 24hr warranty.

Cons:
You may need to drive some distance with no true idea of whether it will be worth your while. You may only get limited information beforehand and some of that may be open to question. You

Unusual specials sell for less.

will probably not be able to test drive the car or even start it up, although by arriving early on preview day you may be able to see the car unloaded and witness what lengths the seller has to go to in order to coax it to life. The cars are often less than showroom clean.

Admission is normally by catalogue for two people, so take a friend. Even if you've tracked down your dream model you need to decide your personal price limit and stop bidding once it goes over, with your friend reminding you to stop, if necessary! Failing to do so can mean paying well over the odds and, since the buyer's premium increases pro-rata, any problems with the car will seem all the more annoying.

Full tools and documents boost value.

Catalogue prices and payment details
Each auction house publishes terms and conditions and spells out charges and acceptable payment methods in their catalogue. These normally give price estimates for most lots, and full or immediate part-payment or a deposit are usually requested, with the balance payable within 24 hours. Look at the small print for cash and credit card limits, and options, such as personal cheques or debit cards or bank drafts. The car won't be released

until paid for, with storage at your cost until completion.

Preview day

Many specialist auctions hold preview days where you can examine the cars outside of the feverish auction atmosphere. Auction staff or sellers may start the cars or show you around, and you are permitted to look underneath but not jack the car up yourself, so take a torch and possibly a mirror on a stick for a better view.

Check the auction car park for bargains.

Auction day

Cars are sold in order of lot number so get there earlier for low number lots. Phrases such as "It's with me at ..." mean the car hasn't yet reached reserve. "It's for sale at ..." means the car has reached reserve and will now sell to the highest bidder. Cars still unsold when the hammer drops may be open to offers via the auctioneer.

eBay & the internet

eBay and other online auctions cover the best and the worst of the auction spectrum. It may be possible to bid across continents yet have a trusted person inspect the car in person and report back to you. Owner's clubs and groups such as jag-lovers.org are ideal for this, although you should offer payment for their time or expenses and decide that you will trust their advice.

If you're bidding very low and do not mind the resultant car being poor because you have risked so little, then you are on safer ground. The author has bought several cheap Jaguars sight unseen and not been disappointed. Tread warily, however!

Most on-line sources show the seller's location, and may even allow you to search by distance from home, which can be useful. Always check, however, that the car is actually at the seller's location. It's usually best to choose your upper limit and bid that at the outset.

Remember, too, that it will be very difficult to obtain satisfaction if a dishonest seller disappears with your money, or a car never arrives because it never existed.

Auctioneers

Barrett-Jackson www.barrett-jackson.com
Bonhams www.bonhams.com
British Car Auctions BCA) www.bca-europe.com or www.british-car- auctions.co.uk
Christies www.christies.com
Coys www.coys.co.uk
eBay www.ebay.com
H&H www.handh.co.uk
RM Sotheby's www.rmsothebys.com
Shannons www.shannons.com.au
Silver www.silverauctions.com

The importance of evidence

You may be more interested in cars than piles of paper, but, buying or selling, good history files not only make interesting reading, but add significantly to the car's resale value. Budget cars with no paperwork may be OK, but any car which has supposedly been rebuilt but has no evidence should be discounted as if it had only minimal work done. The seller may be convincing to you but when you come to sell the car, you will not seem very convincing to the next person. These cars were mostly originally bought by companies or wealthy individuals and were properly serviced, but that means little 30 years later after ten owners unable to look after them properly. For the V12s especially, good documentation is almost essential.

Always, always check the serial number.

Registration documents

Beware a private seller who has only just acquired the car they are selling. Why are they selling on so quickly? Lack of ownership certification normally means extra care is needed with the seller. Where documents do exist, check that the serial numbers actually match the car. Sellers should issue a signed dated and addressed receipt.

Remember that for foreign-registered cars you or the importer will need to pay duty, and this, plus the title issues, takes

Stickers suggest original paint but are not a secure item.

time and effort to administer. A formal certificate of duty paid avoids this liability.

Roadworthiness certificate

Most administrations require that vehicles are regularly tested to prove that they are safe to use. Tests are usually carried out at approved locations and old certificates can confirm the car's history – especially mileage. The best cars are roadworthy with full paperwork and able to be test driven.

Road licence

Many countries have an age-related exemption or reduction in taxes. XJ cars were first sold in 1968, and the early models at least, therefore, qualify for most such systems of reduced taxation. Depending on the savings available, this can help the value of cars older than the cut-off date.

Changed legislation in the UK means that the seller of a car must surrender any existing road fund licence, and it is the responsibility of the new owner to re-tax the vehicle at the time of purchase and before the car can be driven on the road. It's therefore vital to see the Vehicle Registration Certificate (V5C) at the time of purchase, and to have access to the New Keeper Supplement (V5C/2), allowing the buyer to obtain road tax immediately.

If the car is untaxed because it has not been used for a period of time, the owner has to inform the licensing authorities, otherwise the vehicle's date-related registration number will be lost and there will be a painful amount of paperwork to get it re-registered.

Certificates of authenticity

Jaguar Heritage (www.jaguarheritage.com) provides Production Record Trace Certificates for a small fee to those who can prove ownership and supply the four key serial numbers (chassis, body, engine and gearbox), shown on the car's ID plate. The certificate confirms if those numbers belong together, and shows despatch date, model type, original colours, original distributor, and sometimes the first owner and registration number.

If the car has been used in European classic car rallies it may have a FIVA (Fédération International des Véhicules Anciens) certificate. This enables organisers and participants to recognise whether or not a particular vehicle is suitable for individual events. For a certificate go to www.fbhvc.co.uk or www.fiva.org.

Valuation certificate

The seller may have a valuation certificate stating how much the car is worth. Such documents are usually needed for 'agreed value' insurance but should act only as confirmation of your own assessment, rather than a guarantee of value, because the expert has probably not even seen the car. See Chapter 16 for organizations providing valuations.

Service & restoration history

Most cars restored in recent years will have an extensive history file, and many such files use digital photographs. See if the seller will email these to you in advance. For V12s especially, try to get the details of any engine rebuilder or service establishment and call them direct to get their opinion of what was done and what needs doing in future. Make it a condition of purchase that you receive at least copies of photographs, if not originals, to build your own history file with no gaps.

Items like the original bill of sale, handbook, parts invoices and repair or parts bills all add to the story of the car. Even a correct brochure for the car's model year, or original contemporary road tests are useful documents.

Previous ownership records

Due to the introduction of important new legislation on data protection, it is no longer possible to acquire, from the British DVLA, a list of previous owners of a car you own, or are intending to purchase. This scenario will also apply to dealerships and other specialists, from who you may wish to make contact and acquire information on previous ownership and work carried out.

Condition

If the car is suitable you should offer a price based on the asking price adjusted by your findings (Chapter 9). Allow for repairing any faults and use price guides in the classic car press to inform your offer based on whatever condition 'your' car is in.

To back up your offer, use auction values reported in the press, or eBay prices (which are often helpfully low). For a non-standard car you'll need to decide which deviations from standard enhance the price and which detract from it.

Desirable options/extras

These are not rare cars, so there's little need to keep them all perfectly original, and good prices may be asked for cars that differ considerably from catalogue specification. There is a market for cars that are totally standard, but many buyers are happy to see changes, such as an interior adapted from a more upmarket model like a Daimler or Vanden Plas, or even an engine and four-speed automatic from an XJ40. For some, anything non-standard on the car, or missing, reduces the value. Others who like to use their cars may prefer sensible enhancements, such as a later HE engine or S3 injection engine in S1 or S2 twelves and sixes, respectively.

Older cars look best on steel wheels, but Kent alloys came in early and were used on the final V12s so look OK on almost any XJ. Pepperpots also look nice, especially on later cars. Spoke wheels are rare and look odd on all but coupés, perhaps.

Stainless exhausts are common upgrades, whether standard pattern or performance versions, such as AJ6 Engineering's dyno-proven extractor systems for 6 or 12s.

All V12s had electronic ignition, as did late S2 and all S3 sixes. Many other cars have been upgraded, for ease of maintenance/ reliability as much as performance. There are handling upgrades available from specialists, such as Harvey Bailey in the UK or Classic Jaguar in the USA, but the saloons are never going to be sports cars, so good condition standard suspension is fine, with polybushes (especially on the steering rack) being one of the few common changes.

A smaller steering

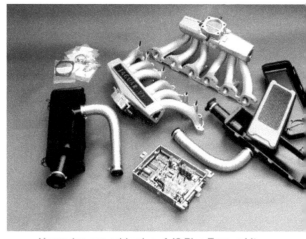

Upgrades can add value: AJ6 Plus Torque kit.

wheel can firm up the steering slightly, and a nice wooden Moto Lita or Nardi wheel is normally desirable (if marginally less safe).

A manual conversion is not everyone's choice for a luxury car but generally is worth having if fuel economy and performance are higher on your list than convenience or purchase price. New standard cooling system parts are the best options, but some custom parts can help, although many others do little to improve cooling, and may actually harm it. The V12 has a complex cooling system with twin thermostats, so careless substitution of custom parts can upset the flow balance and cause unusual cooling problems.

Halogen lights, standard on S3, are good upgrades for earlier cars, as is a modern single-wire alternator and fuses, if cleaning standard fuses is a chore. Liquefied gas fuelling conversions (provided a petrol system is left in place) can dramatically reduce running costs, but are not a common upgrade on pre-1990s cars. Air conditioning is a common fitment for North American and high-spec models, and helps turn the car into a viable daily driver today, although some in temperate climates resent the extra weight, complexity, and fuel cost.

Period original items good for concours.

Conversions usually detract value.

Undesirable features

Matching numbers are not really important except for rare models, and, in fact, most buyers don't care as long as the car is basically as it should be. Some buyers love the VDP and coupé vinyl roof or Webasto folding sunroof, whilst others feel they ruin the car. Converted former automatics are normally worth less than original manuals but more than automatics. Fibreglass wings or other panels are a big turn-off except on a racing conversion, and velour or cloth interiors do not sell as well as leather. Screen leaks and dropped headlinings knock thousands off a car's value and are worth fixing before sale. Certain '70s colours, such as browns and pinks, do not sell as well as metallics, especially reds, blues or any dark colour, though any paint in poor condition is a turn-off.

Some extras help a sale but add little value.

ABS on very late S3 V12s only.

– it'll take longer and cost more than you think

XJ series cars are fast, luxurious and heavy. They need to be sound, solid and, if repaired, then well-repaired. This puts them into a different class from a small 'cooking' saloon which could only manage 65mph when new and is never likely to be highly-stressed or catch an owner out due to spiraling costs or complexity of repair. If you have never restored a car before, you would be well-advised to learn the necessary skills on something simpler and cheaper and less highly-stressed.

Because XJs have always been 'aspirational' purchases for many, there are a lot of cars sold on emotion, having an apparently clean exterior which hides a rotten core dressed up to sell. If you

Definitely worth it! One of only 407 Daimler V12 Coupés.

already have such a car, or have decided to buy one in need of serious work, ask yourself whether it makes sense. The cars are rarely if ever worth what they cost to restore so it normally makes far more sense to buy one in decent condition and avoid major work. By the same token, you should think twice before taking on a car with, for example, a great and inviting interior or engine but with terminal rot below the waist line. One look into the leather and wood interior of a clean car can cause buyers to be over-optimistic about the scope and difficulty of the metalwork repairs which may lie hidden under apparently superficial rust.

Whilst the XK 6-cylinder engines are not too hard to work on, the big V12 is bulky and complex and can swallow a lot of specialist hours to refurbish properly. Think about the type of work you are realistically capable of and calculate the likely budget for a professional doing the other repairs. Then double it since you are likely to overspend heavily. Some people love engines or electrics but can't do structural body work or paint. Be realistic and recognize that it's easy to over-commit, especially if you've a definite schedule in mind for the car to be ready. Good specialist workshops are usually booked up in advance and are not cheap.

Even for those buying an XJ for the pleasure of restoration as a hobby, you

This Greensand Daimler is too far gone to buy.

Can you produce this level of bodywork?

should choose carefully from the many cars out there in need of repair. The ideal is to buy an abandoned project where somebody has already taken care of the aspects you dislike and left the elements you enjoy most as the ones that need finishing.

Budget for some special tools – chassis or powertrain. For example, the big V12 weighs around 700lb, which is more than many normal engine stands can safely manage.

Beware 'shipwright's disease', whereby the more parts you refurbish, the more you come across which are now comparatively sub-standard and you decide to replace those also. At least there's a thriving trade in secondhand spares which are very plentiful and in many cases extremely good value. Some people would even replace the engine

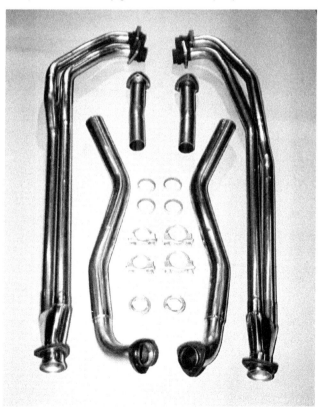

or transmission with a reasonable-appearing secondhand one rather than invest time or money in a full rebuild. This is riskier but for a daily driver non-concours car it's one reasonable option. The cars are not so rare that the whole project cannot be abandoned and a better car sought, with the original serving as a donor for spares, or sold off piecemeal.

More nice kit: an AJ6 extractor exhaust.

XJ cars have large areas of shiny paint, the curves and reflections of which are a vital part of the car's appeal. Paint flaws spoil an XJ more than lesser cars. Some of the most vulnerable panels are detachable and accessible from both sides, so it ought to be simple enough to ensure a good paint job. However, in many cases corners are cut and the car exits the paintshop with superficially good paint that later gives trouble in one of the classic ways described below.

Vinyl roof problems
Not strictly a paint problem but just as troublesome. All standard coupés and many Daimler/VDPs had a seamed vinyl roof covering. This can split, crack, come unstitched, or trap water and leak past screen seals where they wrap under the rubber. Many owners elect to strip them off completely, but for a 'period correct' look professional repair is needed.

Paul Novak's '84 paint damage.

Cracking
For a time, Jaguar used thermoplastic paints, baked after application to 'flow' into a mirror finish requiring no further polishing. Sadly, over time many paints have suffered in extreme climates and for non-original paint all bets are off. Severe cracking is often caused by too heavy an application of paint (or filler beneath). For two-pack modern finishes insufficient stirring of the paint before application can lead to the components being improperly mixed, resulting in cracking. Incompatibility with the paint already on the panel can have a similar effect. Rectification requires stripping entirely or rubbing down to a sound finish before re-spraying.

Orange peel
This is as an uneven paint surface looking like a dimpled orange skin, caused by atomized paint droplets not flowing into each other on the painted surface. It's sometimes possible to polish out with paint cutting compound or very fine abrasive paper on a soft block. A re-spray is necessary in severe cases so consult a bodywork repairer/paint shop for advice. If the paint is two-pack, it will be very hard to flatten.

Classic orange peel on an S1.

Crazing
Sometimes the paint takes on a crazed rather than a cracked appearance. This problem can also be caused by a reaction between the underlying surface and the paint. Paint removal and re-spraying the problem area is usually the only solution. Factory paints can craze in desert climates or sometimes even

Luke Crowe's crazed car.

in milder environments, normally worst on horizontal panels.

Blistering

Almost always caused by corrosion of the metal beneath the paint. Usually perforation will be found in the metal and the damage will almost always be far worse on an XJ than suggested by the area of blistering, especially near the sills. The metal will have to be repaired before repainting.

Micro blistering

Usually the result of an economy re-spray where inadequate heating or too long in primer coat has allowed moisture to penetrate the primer before top coat spraying. Consult a paint specialist, but usually damaged paint will have to be removed before partial or full re-spraying. Also caused by car covers that don't 'breathe' and encourage moisture absorbtion.

Microblistering on an S2.

Fading

Some colours, especially reds, fade under strong sunlight even with polish protection. Sometimes paint restorers or cutting compounds can restore colour, but a re-spray may be the only solution if you're unhappy driving a car with serious 'patina'.

Clouding/peeling

Often a problem with metallic paintwork when the clear lacquer becomes UV damaged or peels off. Poorly applied paint may also peel. The remedy is to strip and start again!

Dimples

Dimples or craters in the paintwork are caused by residues of polish (particularly silicone) not being removed properly before re-spraying. Paint removal and repainting is the only solution – localized if possible, extensive if necessary. Remember, this problem was caused by insufficient care in the first place.

Dents

Small dents are usually easily cured by a 'Dentmaster', or equivalent technician, who can pull or push out the dent (if the paint surface is still intact). Companies offering dent removal services usually come to your home: consult your telephone directory or ask at a local prestige car dealer for personal recommendation.

– just like their owners, XJs need exercise!

Large thirsty 'hobby' cars like the XJ tend to be kept for high days and holidays, which is a shame because they have always been capable of high mileages and everyday, year-round use (with appropriate anti-corrosion care). A run of at least ten miles, once a week, is recommended for the XJ, but is barely adequate for the bigger engines which are so under-stressed. Try for longer runs and avoid frequently starting the engine and switching off before totally hot, as this is worse than never running the car. The large engines take some warming, and failure to disperse acidic combustion byproducts will damage even a fine motor. Depending on storage

Stored cars should be exercised often.

conditions, the interior leather can also benefit from feeding while out of use.

Seized or sluggish components

The XJ has either 3-piston or 4-piston Girling front calipers and twin-piston calipers at the rear, all of which are the modern style with seals fixed in the body and sliding on the piston surfaces rather than vice-versa, as with earlier Jaguar Dunlop brakes. This helps reduce, but does not avoid, corrosion damage or seizure of the working surfaces during prolonged storage. The best way to maintain brakes is to use them and change the fluid prior to extended lay-up. Stainless pistons or some aftermarket calipers may suffer less, but regular fluid changes still help. The master and servo cylinders are conventional but can corrode or fill with

Cable lubed and handbrake left off.

slime from old fluid or deteriorated rubber. The handbrake mechanism and cable should be lubricated, although many cables are nylon lined. Flex hoses to the front calipers and rear suspension cage can crack with age and should be inspected in any car after prolonged storage. Early cars using leather output shaft seals in the differential can also begin to seep on prolonged standing.

For manual transmission cars the clutch friction plate may seize to the pressure plate or flywheel because of corrosion, so regularly working through the gears and easing the clutch to and fro whilst the engine warms up totally is a must, if it is not practicable to take the car for a run because of the season.

Fluids

Old, acidic engine oil will corrode bearings and machined surfaces, as will 'fresh' oil repeatedly loaded with combustion byproducts and condensates from briefly starting up a large, cold Jaguar engine. Check for a 'mayonnaise' appearance under the filler cap or dipstick. Automatic cars benefit from a change to fresh fluid with fresh corrosion inhibitors before a long lay-up.

Old antifreeze or plain water will ruin both XK and V12 water passages and cooling system surfaces, and create serious overheating problems if the cooling system is neglected or excessive scale or sealant sludge collects in the radiator. Lack of antifreeze can cause core plugs to be pushed out or crack the block or head, but this is rarer with the V12 which uses an open-deck block with fewer core plugs. Brake fluid absorbs water from the atmosphere and should be renewed every two years. Old fluid with high water content causes brake failure if the water turns to steam vapour near hot braking components, usually the rear discs first where the pipes can come very close to the exhaust as well as the heat from the shrouded discs and diff.

Since all XJ models have power steering, this fluid too could be changed before a long lay-up although generally the risk of damage is low. Windscreen washer fluid can grow all manner of algae if plain water is used and left alone for months. This can blocks pipes and/or the pump.

Tyres can develop flat spots.

Tyres

Tyres that take the weight of the car in a single position for long periods will develop flat spots. Tyre walls may crack or bulge. Tyres have an approximate life span of 6-8 years depending on conditions. Regular use helps preserve them by dispersing the plasticisers throughout the compound. Avoid exposing the tyres to high temperatures and strong sunlight, and replace poor tyres on a car as heavy and powerful as an XJ. Ask a local tyre specialist how to decipher your tyre's date codes, which vary by country.

Shock absorbers (dampers)

With lack of use, the dampers can corrode on the piston rod. Creaking, groaning, stiff suspension and leaks are signs of this problem.

Rubber and plastic

Radiator hoses can perish and split, possibly resulting in loss of all coolant. The upper right hose from the thermostat to the radiator tends to be the first to harden, but there are very many hoses for oil, water, vacuum and brake fluid that can deteriorate from heat or ozone or solvents or just hardening with age. The injector hoses from the fuel rail are prime candidates, and modern fuels can accelerate hardening and leaks. Don't forget the distributor breathers and fuel and engine breather hoses, even in carburetted cars, let alone if fuel injection has been fitted. Window and door seals can harden and leak. Steering and suspension gaiters and wiper blades will also harden eventually, especially at high ambient temperatures or if left outside in strong ultraviolet light. Vinyl roof and screen seal materials also harden with age and on standing in strong sunlight.

Batteries left in place often die.

Electrics

To keep the battery healthy a trickle charger or battery conditioner will be needed – either on or off the car. Earthing/grounding problems are common when the connections have corroded. Old bullet and spade type electrical connectors corrode and may need disconnecting, cleaning and protection (e.g. Vaseline) and wire insulation can crack.

For serious lay-up remove the battery completely.

Exhaust

Exhaust fumes contain water and acids, so mild steel exhausts corrode from the inside when the car is not used, or is shut off before totally warmed up. The XJ has twin exhausts and the surface area is quite large so condensation is an issue if the system is not high-grade stainless. Some low grade magnetic stainless exhausts are liable to rust almost as quickly as aluminized mild steel.

Jaguar – a car for all the family.

16 The Community

– key people, organisations and companies in the XJ world

XJ cars were the mainstay of Jaguar output for twenty years and during that time they built up a large following of owners and dreamers. Today they are still common enough to be priced within reach of dreamers wanting to become owners at last, or former owners wishing to relive the experience.

Not surprisingly, XJs are also a major part of the current excellent Jaguar club scene. Plenty of cars are still doing duty as daily drivers for people to whom they are just an old car, but enough are in the hands of enthusiasts that a range of specialists exists to serve the market – as well as many cars in breaker's yards as a ready source of secondhand parts.

There is a dedicated forum to all XJ models on the internet at www.jag-lovers.org and you can search the archives or ask questions and receive excellent advice.

Clubs

Jaguar Drivers' Club
18 Stuart Street, Luton, Bedfordshire, LU1 2SL, Tel: +44 (0)1582 419332, www.jaguardriver.co.uk
Set up with factory support originally and covering the full range of Jaguars. Has a good web site, excellent magazine and much XJ support, insurance schemes and offers valuations etc. Extensive overseas network.

Jaguar Enthusiasts' Club
Abbeywood Office Park, Emma Chris Way, Filton, Bristol, BS34 7JU, Tel: +44 (0)1179 698186, www.jec.org.uk
World's largest Jaguar club, offering the usual good magazine as well as tool hire, specially-commissioned spares and events for every taste. Also very useful JagAds internet and print-based advertisement facility.

Jaguar Clubs of North America
c/o Deanie Kennedy, 8137 Zang Street, Arvada, CO-80005
www.jcna.com
Good web site, technical articles and US club network and events calendar. An umbrella organisation for the network of local and regional clubs in the USA.

Jag-Lovers
www.jag-lovers.org
Excellent web-only resource, with great on-line books and discussion forums for early and late XJs and their respective 6 and 12 cylinder engines. Join now and donate a percentage of what it saves you – worth every penny.

Jaguar Heritage
Unit 4 Fairfield Court, Seven Stars Industrial Estate, Wheler Road, Coventry, CV3 4LJ, Tel: +44 (0) 24 7656 1690, www.jaguarheritage.com
Holders of the official Jaguar archives on production numbers, build configuration

and dispatch details, sometimes including first owner information. Sponsored by the Jaguar company in the USA and UK to supply manuals etc and Heritage Certificates confirming the originality of your car's major components.

Parts suppliers
SNG Barratt Group Ltd.
UK, USA, Holland, France and Germany addresses. See www.sngbarratt.com
Biggest and best? One of the oldest and most comprehensive spares sources for Jaguars. Bases in USA/UK/Europe including major remanufacturing capability for electrical parts, sub-assemblies, castings and fabricated parts. Much of what is sold by others comes originally from Barratts.

Martin Robey
Pool Road, Camphill Industrial Estate, Nuneaton, CV10 9AE, Tel: +44 (0)1203 386903, www.martinrobey.co.uk
The main supplier of XJ body panels, having invested in major sheet metal presses and other production facilities. Also holds large spares stocks for other models.

XKs Unlimited
850 Fiero Lane, San Luis Obispo, CA 93401, USA, Tel 805 544 7864, www.xks.com
Good West Coast supplier with clear line drawings in catalogue and website ordering system.

Terry's Jaguar Parts
117 E. Smith Street, Benton, IL 62812, USA, Tel: 1-800 851 9438, www.terrysjag.com
Mid West specialist with good performance parts range

Classic Jaguar
9916 Highway 290W, Austin, TX 78736, USA, Tel: 512 288 8800, www.classicjaguar.com
Wide range of parts and upgrades. Runs own web forum.

Useful books
The XJ Bumper to Bumper
Author: Jim Isbell. Available as a free download from www.jag-lovers.org and extremely useful for S1 through to S3 XJ models. Best downloaded complete and then printed in sections as and when required.

Jagcare III
Author: Dr Gregory Andrachuck. Another free download from www.jag-lovers.org and extremely useful for S3 cars especially. Contains many scanned photographs by Doug Dwyer which increases the overall file size but the full-page pictures can be removed prior to printing if needed.

The XJ-S Book
Author: Kirbert Palm and contributors. The third free download from Jag-Lovers and regarded by many as the definitive collection of all things V12, at least in terms of the engine itself. Written for the XJ-S rather than the XJ but a 'must-read' for learning about the world's longest-running V12 production engine. In case you haven't got the message – join Jag-Lovers free now and donate a fraction of what it saves you to ensure this volunteer site continues to help others.

Haynes Manuals:
Jaguar & Daimler Owner's Workshop Manual (#242)
ISBN 1850101787
Authors: J H Haynes and Peter G Strasman
Hardback: 310pp
Possibly best general guide apart from factory publications for all 6-cylinder cars. Includes 100-page S3 supplement chapter.

Jaguar & Daimler 12-cylinder Owner's Workshop Manual
ISBN 1850102775
Author: Peter G Strasman
Hardback: 410pp
Good practical guide, possibly the best all round apart from the factory publications, for 1968 to 1992 12-cylinder XJ cars, plus information on XJS models. Includes 70-page thirteenth chapter as a supplement purely on the later models.

Jaguar XJ6 Restoration Manual (#H4020)
ISBN 1844250202
Author: Dave Pollard
Hardback: 214pp
Good general guide on history and restoration of the XJ cars apart from V12s. Not a full workshop manual, but excellent photos. Recommended.

6-cylinder XJ production (Jaguar, Daimler/VDP combined)

	2.8	3.4	4.2 swb	4.2 Coupé	4.2 lwb
S 1	22,555	–	70,599	–	1260
S 2	170	9331	14,582	8164	72,155
S 3	–	5799	–	–	146,878

12-cylinder XJ production (Jaguar, Daimler/VDP combined)

	5.3 swb	5.3 Coupé	5.3 lwb	Total
S 1	3008	–	1105	4113
S 2	–	2262	20,344	22,606
S 3	–	–	24,566	24,566

There are some small discrepancies between alternative sources for the above numbers, which are often split between various models and markets. The overall balance of production, however, is as indicated.

Technical specifications by model

Specifications changed between years, models and markets so only an indicative summary is possible here. Please check appropriate information for specific models/years/markets from other sources, such as original brochures found at www.jag-lovers.org.

Series 1 XJ6 & variants – produced 1968-1973

2.8 engine: in-line 6-cylinder DOHC, 2792cm^3, 83 x 86mm, 180bhp @ 6000rpm and 182lb/ft @ 3750rpm, CR 9:1

4.2 engine: in-line 6-cylinder DOHC, 4235cm^3, 92.07 x 106mm, 245bhp @ 5500rpm and 283lb/ft @ 3750rpm, CR 8:1

5.3 engine: V12 cylinder SOHC, 5343cm^3, 90 x 70mm, 253bhp @ 6000rpm and 301lb/ft @ 3500rpm, CR 9:1

Transmission (manual, 6-cylinder): 4-speed all synchro gearbox, with or without Laycock de Normanville overdrive

Transmission (automatic): Borg Warner 3-speed Type 35 (2.8L), Model 8 (4.2L) or Model 12 (V12). Axle ratio 2.8L: 4.27:1 (3.54 with overdrive). 4.2L: 3.54 (3.07 with overdrive). 5.3L: 3.31

Length: 15ft 9.25in (4810mm). Width: 5ft 9in (1750mm). Height: 4ft 6in (1370mm)

Unladen weight: 32-34cwt (1626-1727kg) depending on model

Suspension: Fully independent all round, incorporating anti-dive geometry, mounted on rubber-isolated subframes front and rear, with front anti-roll bar

Steering: Power-assisted via vane pump, 3.5 turns lock-to-lock, 16in diameter steering wheel, collapsible and telescopically adjustable column

Brakes: Vacuum servo-assisted discs all round, with independent circuits, pressure distribution valve and self-adjusting handbrake on the inboard rear discs

Wheels: Silver painted 15 x 7in steel wheels or vented steel pattern on last S1 XJ12s. 205/70/VR15 radial tyres

Generally as for S1 but with 3.4-litre engine replacing the 2.8, ventilated front discs, improved styling and heating/ventilation, etc. Fuel injection and electronic ignition on late S2 North American models (4.2 & 5.3L). See brochures for more detail.

Standardised on the long wheelbase platform with new Pininfarina-influenced body with the following dimensions:
Length: 16ft 2.25in (4950mm).
Width: 5ft 9.25in (1760mm).
Height: 4ft 6in (1370mm)
Unladen weight: c. 34cwt (1676kg) depending on model
The high-efficiency (HE) V12 was introduced in 1981 and full catalyst emission equipment, anti-lock brakes, fuel computers and other refinements were added during production. For detailed specifications see catalogues.

The Essential Buyer's Guide™ series ...

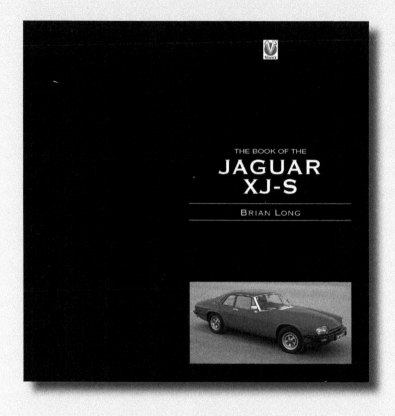

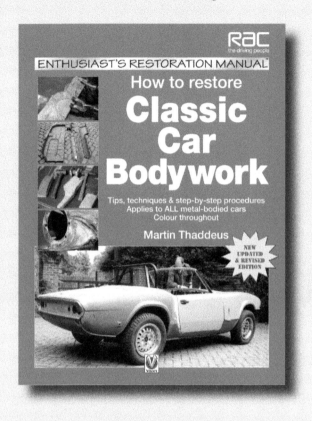

Index